The Countries

Dominican Republic

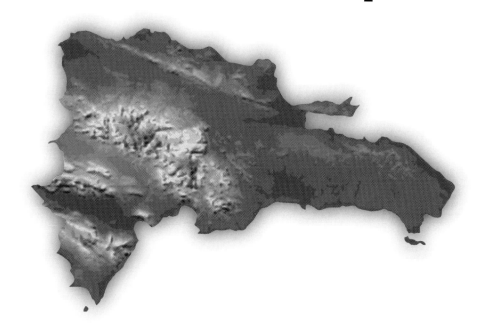

Kate A. Furlong

ABDO Publishing Company

visit us at
www.abdopub.com

Published by ABDO Publishing Company, 4940 Viking Drive, Suite 622, Edina, Minnesota 55435. Copyright © 2000 Abdo Consulting Group, Inc., Pentagon Tower, P.O. Box 36036, Minneapolis, Minnesota 55435 USA. International copyrights reserved in all countries. No part of this book may be reproduced in any form without written permission from the publisher.

Printed in the United States.

Interior Photos: Paul Gerace (pgs. 5, 14, 16, 21, 22, 24, 28, 29, 33, 34, 35 [top], 36 [top], 37)
                Corbis (pgs. 9, 11, 12, 18, 19, 25, 27, 31, 35 [bottom], 36 [bottom])
                AP/Wideworld (pg. 13)
Editors: Bob Italia, Tamara L. Britton
Art Direction & Maps: Pat Laurel
Cover & Interior Design: MacLean & Tuminelly (Mpls.)

Library of Congress Cataloging-in-Publication Data

Furlong, Kate A.,1977-
    Dominican Republic / Kate A. Furlong.
       p. cm. -- (The Countries)
    Includes index.
    ISBN 1-57765-391-2
    1. Dominican Republic--Juvenile literature. [1. Dominican Republic.] I. Title. II. Series.

F1934.2 .F87 2000
972.93--dc21
                                                       00-033215

Contents

¡Hola! 4

Fast Facts 6

Timeline 7

Growth of an Island Nation 8

Island in the Sea 14

Plants & Animals 18

Dominicans 20

Turning Crops into Cash 24

Cities Rich in History 26

Moving People and Goods 28

The Dominican Republic's Government 30

Dominican Celebrations 32

Island Fun 34

Glossary 38

Web Sites 39

Index 40

¡Hola!

Dominicans say hello to each other by saying *¡hola!* They live on an island with mountains, beaches, and **subtropical forests**. The land's rich soil and regular rain make it a great place to grow crops. And hundreds of unusual plants and animals make this land their home.

People have lived on the island for thousands of years. After Christopher Columbus discovered it, the island became Spain's first colony in the New World. Spaniards, Indians, and African slaves built the colony and created a Dominican culture.

Dominican culture is rich in spirit. It has its own special kinds of food, art, and sports. And its festivals are some of the best in the West Indies.

The Dominican Republic's **economy** is based on farming. This includes growing crops and processing them. These two **industries** employ more than half of all Dominicans.

The Dominican Republic's cities are some of the oldest in the New World. Many have well-kept colonial buildings. And their busy ports help support the country's economy.

Large ships are an important form of transportation in the Dominican Republic. They carry goods into and out of the country. People travel in small buses and minivans.

The country's government is a republic. Dominicans elect the president and lawmakers. The president, lawmakers, and judges must follow the country's **constitution**.

In its long history, the Dominican Republic has faced many problems. Wars, **dictators**, and a poor **economy** have all made life difficult for Dominicans. Today, the country's 8 million citizens are working hard to improve their lives and their country.

Hola *from the Dominican Republic!*

Fast Facts

OFFICIAL NAME: Dominican Republic (República Dominicana)

CAPITAL: Santo Domingo

LAND
- Mountain Ranges: Cordillera Central, Cordillera Septentrional, Cordillera Oriental
- Highest point: Pico Duarte 10,417 feet (3,175 m)
- Lowest point: Lago Enriquillo -154 feet (-46 m)
- Major River: Río Yaque del Norte
- Largest Lake: Lago Enriquillo

PEOPLE
- Population: 8,129,734 (1999 est.)
- Major Cities: Santo Domingo, Santiago de los Caballeros
- Language: Spanish
- Religion: Roman Catholic

GOVERNMENT
- Form: Republic
- Head: President
- Legislature: National Congress made up of the Senate and the Chamber of Deputies
- Flag: A centered white cross that extends to the edges divides the flag into two red rectangles and two blue rectangles; a small coat of arms is at the center of the cross
- Nationhood: February 27, 1844

ECONOMY
- Agricultural Products: Sugarcane, coffee, cotton, cacao, tobacco, rice, beans, potatoes, corn, bananas, cattle, pigs, dairy products, beef, eggs
- Mining Products: Gold, silver, and ferronickel
- Manufactured Products: Electricity, building materials, light metalwares, textiles, paper, glass and wood products, and food and beverages
- Money: Peso (one peso equals one hundred *centavos*)

SANTO DOMINGO

Dominican Republic's Flag

A Dominican bill worth 10 pesos

Timeline

3,000 B.C.	People first arrive in Hispaniola
A.D. 300	Arawak Indians move to Hispaniola
1492	Christopher Columbus discovers Hispaniola; Spain establishes a colony there
1697	France controls western Hispaniola, creating Haiti
1795	France controls of all of Hispaniola
1804	Haiti gains independence from France
1809	Spain again controls its colony in Western Hispaniola
1821	The Dominican Republic wins its independence from Spain; Haiti overtakes the Dominican Republic
1844	The Dominican Republic wins independence from Haiti
1916	The U.S. sends Marines to the Dominican Republic to create peace among the political groups
1930	Rafael Trujillo comes to power
1961	The Dominican Republic's army assassinates Trujillo
1963	The Dominican Republic holds its first free elections
1965	A civil war breaks out; the U.S. occupies the Dominican Republic to create peace
1979	Hurricane David wrecks much of the country
2000	Hipolito Mejia elected president

Growth of an Island Nation

The Dominican Republic and Haiti are on an island called Hispaniola. It has been home to several native peoples. The Taíno were Arawak Indians who lived there. They were peaceful people who farmed, hunted, and lived in villages.

The Caribs came to Hispaniola after the Taíno. The Caribs were excellent sailors and warriors. They used canoes to move among the West Indies, conquering other groups. They even tried to conquer the peaceful Taíno.

In 1492, Christopher Columbus discovered Hispaniola. Soon, Spain established a colony and built cities there. The colonists liked Hispaniola. It had rich **mines** and good farmland.

After the colonists arrived, life became hard for the Taíno and Carib Indians. The Spaniards used them as slaves. And many died from diseases and lack of food. By 1550, there were few Taíno or Carib Indians left in Hispaniola. So, the Spaniards brought in African slaves to take their place.

During this time, the island's cities grew. They had the New World's first **cathedral**, hospital, **monastery**, and university. But soon, many settlers left Hispaniola in search of even richer lands, such as Mexico and Peru. With fewer settlers, Hispaniola became weak.

Britain, France, and the Netherlands attacked Hispaniola. Pirates attacked Hispaniola, too. Spain began to lose its control over the island. In 1697, France took control of western Hispaniola. France named this part of the island Saint-Domingue. The name was later changed to Haiti.

Upon landing in the New World, Columbus met the Taíno and Carib Indians.

Haiti had great success in the 1700s. Its many **sugarcane plantations** brought Haiti power and wealth. But Spain's colony on eastern Hispaniola was still weak. In 1795, France took over Spain's colony. This meant France controlled the whole island.

Haiti won its independence from France in 1804. Five years later, Spain regained control of its colony in eastern Hispaniola. Then, in 1821, Spain's colony won its independence. It formed a country called the Dominican Republic, which spread across central and eastern Hispaniola.

Shortly after the Dominican Republic won its independence, Haiti attacked it. Haiti's president Jean-Pierre Boyer ruled the Dominican Republic. He freed the slaves. But he was also cruel to many people.

In the 1830s, Juan Pablo Duarte created a secret society to fight the Haitians. His group succeeded. And in 1844, the Dominican Republic finally gained true independence.

After winning its freedom, the Dominican Republic faced other problems. **Dictators** ruled the country for many years. Some of the dictators improved the roads and farms. But the country still had a weak **economy** and much debt.

As time went on, the country's politics grew violent and disorderly. So, in 1916, U.S. president Woodrow Wilson sent the Marines to the Dominican Republic. They worked to bring peace to the country. U.S. troops stayed in the Dominican Republic until 1924.

After U.S. troops left, Dominicans elected a new president named Horacio Vásquez. Soon, the people disliked him. They did not think he was a skilled leader. In 1930, there was a **revolt** against Vásquez. The revolt succeeded and dictator Rafael Trujillo took control.

Trujillo ruled the Dominican Republic for 31 years. Under Trujillo, the **economy** grew and politics remained stable. But he controlled every part of the country, from the church to the military. Citizens could not speak out against Trujillo or his government. In 1961, members of the Dominican Republic's army **assassinated** Trujillo.

Rafael Trujillo

*U.S. troops move through
Santo Domingo in 1965.*

After Trujillo's death, Dominicans tried to establish a **democracy**. In 1963, they held the country's first free elections. They elected Juan Bosch president. Bosch wanted to create a strong government and political freedom. But after only seven months, a political group overthrew him and took control.

The new government did not have much success. In 1965, military officers started a civil war. The U.S. worried that a **communist** group might take over. So, in 1965, the U.S. occupied the Dominican Republic once again.

In 1966, Dominicans elected a new president named Joaquín Balaguer. He ruled for 12 years. During this time, the **economy** improved and the country grew.

During the 1970s and 1980s, the country began to face problems. Hurricane David hurt much of the country in 1979.

And the **economy** weakened. Debt and **inflation** grew. People started striking against the government.

Today, the Dominican Republic is still trying to solve its many problems. On May 19, 2000, Dominicans elected a new president named Hipolito Mejia. He is working to improve the lives of all Dominicans.

President Hipolito Mejia (right) poses with his running mate, Milagros Ortiz.

Island in the Sea

The Dominican Republic has 800 miles (1,288 km) of coastline.

The Dominican Republic is on the island of Hispaniola. It is part of the West Indies. They are a group of islands between North and South America. These islands separate the Caribbean Sea and the Atlantic Ocean. Hispaniola is the second-largest island in the West Indies. Only Cuba is larger.

Haiti is the Dominican Republic's closest neighbor. It lies on the western third of Hispaniola. Florida is 670 miles (1,078 km) northwest of the Dominican Republic. Colombia and Venezuela are 310 miles (500 km) to its south. A **channel** called the Mona Passage separates the Dominican Republic from Puerto Rico.

The Dominican Republic has several mountain ranges. The Cordillera Central mountain range runs through the country's center. This range has Pico Duarte. At 10,417 feet (3,175 m), it is the highest mountain in the West Indies. Other important mountain ranges are the Cordillera Septentrional and the Cordillera Oriental.

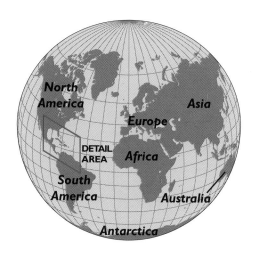

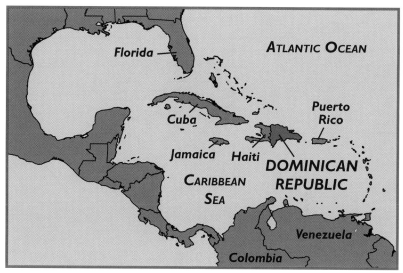

Between the Cordillera Central and the Cordillera Septentrional lies the Cibao Valley. The east-central part of the Cibao Valley has a plain called the Vega Real. It has some of the richest soil in the West Indies.

The Dominican Republic has many lakes and rivers. The country's longest river is the Río Yaque del Norte. It flows in the northern Dominican

Many plants grow well in the Dominican Republic's rich soil.

Republic. Lago Enriquillo is the country's largest lake. It has salt water instead of fresh water. It is near the Haitian border.

Most of the Dominican Republic has a warm, mild climate. The average temperate is 77° F (25° C). Temperatures get cooler at higher elevations. The country's western region is dry. The rest of the land gets plenty of rain. The rainy season runs from May to November.

Hurricanes and tropical storms are a danger to the Dominican Republic. These storms usually strike between August and October. They have high winds and heavy rain. When they strike land, these storms can wreck buildings and kill people.

Rainfall

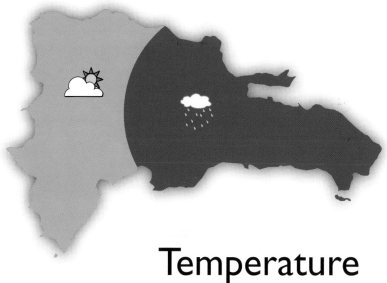

AVERAGE YEARLY RAINFALL

Inches		Centimeters
40 - 60		*100 - 150*
60 - 80		*150 - 200*

North
West — East
South

Temperature

AVERAGE TEMPERATURE

Fahrenheit		Celsius
68° - 86°		*20° - 30°*
50° - 68°		*10° - 20°*

Winter

Summer

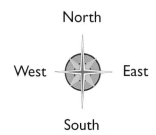

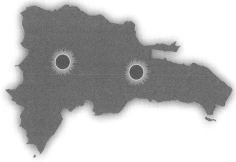

Plants & Animals

Manatees are often called sea cows.

The waters surrounding the Dominican Republic are rich in creatures. Each year about 10,000 humpback whales come to Samaná Bay and Banco de la Plata. Manatees also live in the Dominican Republic's waters. They are slow moving, gentle animals.

More than 400 kinds of birds live in the Dominican Republic. The ruddy duck swims through the country's waters. It has red feathers and a bright blue bill. Flamingos wade in Lago Enriquillo. And the stygian owl watches the forest from beneath feathers that look like eyebrows.

Reptiles live in the country, too. Rhinoceros iguanas live near Lago Enriquillo. They only live on Hispaniola. Lago Enriquillo is also home to alligators and crocodiles.

Rhinoceros iguanas can grow to be three feet (one meter) long.

Over 5,000 kinds of plants grow in the Dominican Republic. **Subtropical forests** cover most of the land. The royal palm is the most common plant in these forests. Mahogany, jaguar palm, ground oak, cashew trees, and yellowwood are common, too.

The Dominican Republic also has mangrove forests. Mangrove forests grow near water. They have shrubs and trees with aboveground roots.

The country has montane forests, too. They grow at 6,500 feet (2,000 m) in elevation. Montane forests have many plants including ferns, orchids, palm trees, and pine trees.

Thick forests cover much of the Dominican Republic.

Over the years, lumberjacks, farmers, and developers have chopped down many of the trees in the montane forests. The tree roots hold the soil in place. Without them, rain washes the soil away. This makes it hard to grow crops and other plants.

The Dominican Republic's few dry areas in the west also have lots of plants. Cactuses, agaves, and thorn trees grow well in these areas.

Dominicans

The Taíno and Carib Indians were some of Hispaniola's first settlers. But after Columbus arrived, disease, war, and slavery killed many of them.

Lots of Spaniards moved to the island after it became a colony. They brought African slaves to work on their plantations. Over time, some Spaniards and Africans had children together. Today, most Dominicans are part Spanish and part African.

Spaniards brought the Spanish language and the Catholic religion to the Dominican Republic. Today, nearly all Dominicans speak Spanish. It is the country's official language. And most Dominicans are Catholic.

Many Dominicans also believe in folk healers. They get advice from Catholic saints. These healers also use herbs and roots to cure people of bad spirits and diseases. **Immigrants** from Haiti practice an African folk religion called voodoo.

Dominicans value families. Dominican families are usually made up of a mother, a father, and several children.

Dominican families enjoy many delicious foods. One of the most common meals is called *la bandera*. It includes white rice, red beans, meat, a salad, and fried **plantains**. Another popular meal is *sancocho de siete carnes*. It is a stew with seven kinds of meat and many vegetables.

Clothing in the Dominican Republic is similar to that worn in the U.S. and Canada. Even though the weather is often hot, shorts and tank tops are worn only at the beach. Men usually wear dress shirts and pants. Lots of women wear dresses, skirts, and blouses. Children usually wear uniforms to school.

Dominican children must attend school from age 7 to age 14. The government provides free schools. Primary school lasts for six years. Then students attend an intermediate school for two years. A four-year school and then college follow this.

Dominican boys wearing typical school uniforms

The Dominican Republic's school system has problems. Few poor students complete all their schooling. There are not enough teachers, school buildings, or funds. And in some rural areas, there are no schools at all.

Another one of the Dominican Republic's biggest problems is housing. Many homes do not have clean water. And the electricity often stops working. Many **plantation** workers live in huts made of palm leaves, bamboo, and mud. And in the cities, some people live in houses made of cardboard, tires, and other scrap material.

Not all homes in the Dominican Republic are rundown. **Traditional** country homes are made of palm and pine boards. They are usually painted in bright colors. In the cities, middle class families live in modern homes like those in the U.S. and Canada.

Colorful, traditional homes line a Dominican beach.

Papaya Batido

Dominicans enjoy drinking cool, fruity drinks called batidos. Batidos can be made with any kind of fruit. One of the most popular kinds of batido is made with papaya.

1 ripe papaya
6 tbsp milk
1 tsp vanilla

5 tbsp lime juice
4 tbsp sugar
2 cups crushed ice

Peel the papaya and remove the seeds. Chop the papaya into cubes. Combine the papaya, milk, lime juice, sugar, vanilla, and ice in a blender. Blend at high speed until mixture is smooth and thick.

AN IMPORTANT NOTE TO THE CHEF: Always have an adult help with the preparation and cooking of food. Never use kitchen utensils or appliances without adult permission and supervision.

LANGUAGE

ENGLISH	SPANISH
Mother _____	Madre
Father _____	Padre
Hello _____	Hola
Good-bye _____	Adiós
Please _____	Por Favor
Thank You _____	Gracias
Yes _____	Sí
No _____	No

Turning Crops into Cash

The Dominican Republic's **economy** is based on farming. Nearly half of all Dominican workers are farmers. They produce much of their country's food. They also **export** some of their crops to other parts of the world.

The country's most important crop is **sugarcane**. It is the Dominican Republic's leading export. Sugarcane is grown on **plantations**. Farmers also grow tobacco, **cacao**, and coffee.

Minerals are another valuable part of the Dominican Republic's economy. They are the country's second-leading export. Gold, silver, and ferronickel are the main minerals **mined**.

Most small Dominican farms still use traditional farming methods.

Industry is starting to grow in the Dominican Republic. The largest industry is sugar production. Workers also process foods and drinks. Some factories make furniture and clothing. These factories have reduced the Dominican Republic's **imports**.

A Dominican sugar-processing mill

Tourism has also become a valuable part of the **economy**. People enjoy visiting the country's historic buildings and beautiful beaches.

The Dominican Republic's economy has problems. The population is growing quickly and there are not enough jobs for everyone. So, some Dominicans **emigrate** to the U.S. to find jobs. They usually send money back to their relatives who still live on the island.

The country's dependence on **sugarcane** causes another problem. When world prices for sugar are low, the economy suffers. To fix this problem, the government has worked to develop manufacturing and **mining**.

Cities Rich in History

The Dominican Republic's capital city is Santo Domingo. Christopher Columbus's brother Bartholomew founded the city in 1496. Today, more than 2 million people live in Santo Domingo. It is Hispaniola's largest city. And it is the first permanent city that Europeans established in the New World.

Santo Domingo is located in the country's southern coast. Its position near the Ozama River and the Caribbean Sea has made it an important shipping city. Santo Domingo's port carries about half of the country's trade.

Santo Domingo is the **industrial** center of the Dominican Republic. Workers produce cement, textiles, **petrochemicals**, and plastics. Santo Domingo has food and metal processing plants, too.

The city is also full of cultural areas. The Zona Colonial has buildings from the city's first settlers. It is also home to the University of Santo Domingo, which is the New World's first university. Along the water, Santo Domingo has a wide, tree-lined street called the Avenida George Washington.

Santiago de los Caballeros is the Dominican Republic's second-largest city. This city is the capital of the Santiago **province**. It is located on the Río Yaque del Norte.

Historians are not sure who founded the city. Some believe Christopher Columbus founded it in 1494. Others believe his brother Bartholomew founded it a year later. But by 1504, *caballeros* (gentlemen) had moved into the city. That is how the city got the last part of its name.

Santiago de los Caballeros is in the Cibao Valley. The valley's rich soil makes crops grow well in and near Santiago. So, the city's **economy** is based on farming. Farmers grow tobacco, **sugarcane**, rice, **cacao**, and coffee.

The Ozama River cuts through Santo Domingo.

Moving People and Goods

Santo Domingo is the Dominican Republic's transportation center. From Santo Domingo, it is easy for people and goods to reach all parts of the country.

These Dominicans are traveling by boat.

Most of the Dominican Republic's goods are **imported** and **exported** in large ships. Southern cities such as Santo Domingo, San Pedro de Macorís, and La Romana have excellent ports. Samaná Bay has one of the largest harbors in the West Indies. Smaller boats ferry people between coastal cities. They also give tours to visitors.

Trucks and trains also transport goods. The railways in the Dominican Republic only carry goods. They do not carry any riders.

Few Dominicans own cars. Instead, they get around in buses, vans, trucks, and motorcycles. Small buses called *gua-guas* run along the highways. On local streets, minivans and trucks called *públicos* move Dominicans from place to place.

Airplanes carry travelers in and out of the Dominican Republic. The national airline is called Dominican Aviation Company. It flies to the U.S. and other countries in the West Indies.

In rural areas, some people live far from good roads. They get from place to place on foot. They also use horses to carry goods and travel.

In the country, some Dominicans use horses to get around.

The Dominican Republic's Government

The Dominican Republic is divided into **29 provinces**. It also has a national district called the Distrito Federal. This is where the central government is located.

The country's government is a republic. It follows the 1966 **Constitution**. This divides the country's power between the president, the National Congress, and the Supreme Court. The constitution promises freedom and human rights. It also allows people over age 18 to vote.

Dominicans elect a president every four years. The president is commander in chief of the military. The president also chooses the governors of the provinces. A vice president and a **cabinet** work with the president.

The National Congress is made up of the Senate and the Chamber of Deputies. These two groups make the country's laws. Voters elect the members of the National Congress.

The Dominican Republic has several courts. The president and lawmakers choose the judges. The country's highest court is the Supreme Court.

Money in the Dominican Republic is called the peso. It can be divided into 100 smaller units, called *centavos*.

The president's office is in the National Palace.

Dominican Celebrations

The Dominican Republic has many holidays and festivals. Dominicans celebrate their national holiday on February 27. It marks their country's independence from Haiti in 1844.

On *Noche Buena* (Christmas Eve), families gather for a big dinner. Later, they sing songs and talk. At midnight, many families attend **mass**. Children don't get gifts until January 6, which is called Kings' Day. They get their gifts from the three kings instead of Santa Claus.

Before Easter, Dominicans celebrate Carnival. It takes place just before **Lent**. Carnival is the country's biggest festival. Men and boys wear colorful masks and costumes. They walk around in the streets, playfully teasing each other. People also dance, listen to music, and watch parades and street plays.

The week before Easter, Sosúa holds a Holy Week festival. Dominicans pack the city. They eat, drink, dance, and relax on the beach.

Merengue Festivals are another popular event. They are held in Santo Domingo and Puerta Plata. Dominicans gather to watch the country's best merengue musicians and dancers perform. The streets are lined with food vendors. And people camp on the beaches and have parties through the night.

Dominicans celebrate other music festivals as well. The Latin Music festival in Santo Domingo has salsa, merengue, *bachata*, and jazz musicians. Puerto Plata's Cultural Festival also has some of Latin America's best musicians. And it also has an arts and crafts fair.

Every June, people head to Cabarate. It is one of the world's best windsurfing sites. Cabarate's Encuentro Classic has windsurfing competitions and classes. At night, people go to parties and concerts on the beach.

Carnival masks represent good and evil.

Island Fun

The Dominican Republic offers its people lots of ways to spend their free time. People can watch sports or dance to lively music. They can also watch television or visit museums to look at Dominican art. Some Dominicans also spend time creating **traditional** crafts.

Baseball is one of the Dominican Republic's most popular sports. Children and adults enjoy playing and watching baseball. The country has produced many excellent players, including Sammy Sosa. And San Pedro de Macorís has produced more major-league players than any other city in the world.

Many young Dominicans enjoy playing baseball.

*A gallera **shortly before a cockfight***

Another popular sport is cockfighting. Nearly every town in the Dominican Republic has a cockfighting pit, called a *gallera*. Two **gamecocks** are put into the *gallera*, where they fight until one dies. Watchers place bets on which gamecock will win. The government disapproves of the sport. But it still remains popular, especially among rural men.

Nearly all Dominicans enjoy dancing to the lively beat of merengue music. Merengue began in the Dominican Republic and is the country's most popular music. It is played on four instruments. One instrument is an accordion. There is also a drum called a *tambora*. An instrument that is scraped is called a *güira*. A wooden box with keys is called a *marimba*.

Musicians playing the güira *(left) and the accordion*

Dominicans also enjoy listening to *bachata*. It is music about country life and lost loves. *Bachata* and merengue are not the only kinds of music heard in the Dominican Republic. People also listen to bolero, salsa, pop, and rock music. In rural areas, **traditional** music with African roots can be heard.

Many Dominicans still enjoy making traditional crafts. They include colorful Carnival masks, ceramic dolls, windchimes, and wood carvings. Some people sell their crafts to **tourists** in the country's markets.

A man sells Dominican crafts in a market.

Dominican crafts are also made of larimar and amber. The Dominican Republic has the only land in the world with larimar. It is a bright, blue-green stone. The Dominican Republic's land also produces the world's best amber. Amber and larimar are both used in jewelry and small, carved objects.

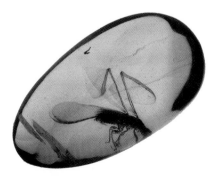

Amber forms when sticky tree resin and oxygen combine. After many years of being buried, the resin gets hard and forms amber. Insects trapped in the resin long ago are sometimes found in amber.

Watching television is another way for Dominicans to relax. The country has seven television stations. Some stations from Miami, Florida, also come through on Dominican television. People like to watch baseball, movies, and soap operas.

The country's many museums display work from Dominican artists. Because of Spain's lasting influence, lots of Dominican art looks Spanish. But a kind of folk art, called primitive art, is gaining popularity. It uses bright colors and simple figures to show everyday life in the country.

The Dominican Republic's colorful art, crafts, music, dance, and sports show the country's spirited personality. They give Dominicans a break from the difficult daily life that many of them face. As they work to improve their country and their lives, the Dominicans' spirit continues to shine through.

Dominican primitive art by painter Eliesel Mercedes

Glossary

assassinate - to kill an important person.

cabinet - a group of people who give a president advice.

cacao - a bean used to make chocolate and cocoa.

cathedral - a large, important church.

channel - a body of water that connects two larger bodies of water.

communism - an economic system in which everything is owned by the government and given to the people as they need it.

constitution - a paper that describes a country's laws and government.

democracy - a form of government where the people hold the power. They elect officials to represent them.

dictator - a ruler who has complete control and usually governs in a cruel or unfair way.

economy - the way a country uses its money, goods, and natural resources.

emigrate - to leave one country and move to another.

export - to send goods to another country for sale or trade.

gamecock - a rooster trained to fight.

immigrant - a person who leaves his or her homeland and moves to another country to live.

import - to bring in goods from another country for sale or trade.

industry - the production of a large number of goods by business and factories.

inflation - a rise in the price of goods and services.

Lent - the forty days before Easter.

mass - a worship ceremony in the Catholic Church.

mine - an underground source of minerals, such as gold or silver.

monastery - a place where religious men called monks live and work.

petrochemical - a chemical made from natural gas.

plantain - a fruit that looks like a large banana but is not as sweet.
plantation - a large farm. Workers who live on the plantation harvest the crops.
province - a political division that is like a state.
revolt - a movement against a state, country, or ruler.
subtropical forest - a forest that grows in an area that has hot, dry summers and cool, moist winters. Subtropical plants usually have thick, waxy leaves to prevent water loss in the hot summers.
sugarcane - a tall grass with thick, juicy stems from which sugar is made.
tourism - the act of touring or traveling for pleasure.
traditional - something that has been passed down from parent to child for many generations.

Web Sites

Dominican Republic: A Country Study
http://lcweb2.loc.gov/frd/cs/dotoc.html
The Library of Congress sponsors this site on the Dominican Republic. It has a lot of information on the Dominican Republic's history, society, economy, government and politics, and military.

CIA: The World Factbooks — Dominican Republic
http://www.odci.gov/cia/publications/factbook/dr.html
This site by the CIA offers up-to-date statistics on the Dominican Republic. It has sections on the Dominican Republic's geography, people, government, economy, communications, transportation, military, and transnational issues.

These sites are subject to change. Go to your favorite search engine and type in "Dominican Republic" for more sites.

Index

A
Africans 4, 8, 20
amber 36
animals 4, 18
art 4, 34, 37

B
bachata 33, 36
Balaguer, Joaquín 12
Banco de la Plata 18
baseball 34
Bosch, Juan 12
Boyer, Jean-Pierre 10

C
Cabarate 33
Carib Indians 8, 20
children 20, 21, 32, 34
climate 16, 21
clothing 21
cockfighting 35
Colombia 14
Columbus, Bartholomew 26, 27
Columbus, Christopher 4, 8, 20, 26, 27
crafts 34, 36, 37
crops 4, 24, 25, 27
Cuba 14

D
dance 32, 33, 34, 35, 37
Duarte, Juan Pablo 10

E
economy 4, 5, 10, 11, 12, 13, 24, 25, 27

F
families 20, 21
festivals 4, 32, 33
Florida 14
food 4, 21
France 9, 10

G
government 5, 11, 12, 13, 30, 31

H
Haiti 8, 9, 10, 14, 16, 20, 32
Hispaniola 8, 9, 10, 14, 18, 20, 26
holidays 32
houses 22
hurricanes 12, 16

I
independence 10, 32
industry 4, 25, 26

L
La Romana 28
Lago Enriquillo 16, 18
language 20
larimar 36

M
Mejia, Hipolito 13
merengue 32, 33, 35, 36
mining 24, 25
money 31
mountains 4, 14, 16
music 32, 33, 34, 35, 36, 37

O
Ozama River 26

P
plants 4, 19
Puerta Plata 32, 33
Puerto Rico 14

R
religion 20, 32
Río Yaque del Norte 16, 27

S
Samaná Bay 18, 28
San Pedro de Macorís 28, 34
Santiago de los Caballeros 27
Santo Domingo 26, 28, 32, 33
school 21, 22
Sosa, Sammy 34
Sosúa 32
Spain 4, 8, 9, 10, 20
sports 4, 34, 35, 37

T
Taíno Indians 8, 20
tourism 25, 36
transportation 5, 28, 29
Trujillo, Rafael 11, 12

U
United States of America 11, 12, 21, 22, 25, 29

V
Vásquez, Horacio 11
Venezuela 14

W
West Indies 4, 8, 14, 16, 28, 29
Wilson, Woodrow 11